i will write to avenge my people

# i will write to avenge my people

*the nobel lecture*

## ANNIE ERNAUX

TRANSLATED BY **ALISON L. STRAYER**

Including:

**OPENING ADDRESS**
*by Professor Carl-Henrik Heldin*

**BANQUET SPEECH**
*by Annie Ernaux*
*translated by Sophie Lewis*

**PRESENTATION SPEECH**
*by Professor Anders Olsson*
*translated by Kim Loughran*

**SEVEN STORIES PRESS**
new york · oakland · london

Opening Address by Professor Carl-Henrik Heldin
© The Nobel Foundation 2022

Nobel Lecture by Annie Ernaux
© The Nobel Foundation 2022

Banquet Speech by Annie Ernaux
© The Nobel Foundation 2022

Presentation Speech by Professor Anders Olsson
© The Nobel Foundation 2022

Seven Stories Press
140 Watts Street
New York, NY 10013
www.sevenstories.com

Library of Congress Cataloging-in-Publication Data is on file

College professors and high school and middle school teachers may order
free examination copies of Seven Stories Press titles. Visit https://www.seven-
stories.com/pg/resources-academics or email academic@sevenstories.com.

Printed in the United States of America

9  8  7  6  5  4  3  2  1

# Contents

Opening Address

PROFESSOR CARL-HENRIK HELDIN

9

Nobel Lecture:
I Will Write to Avenge My People

ANNIE ERNAUX

17

Banquet Speech

ANNIE ERNAUX

33

Presentation Speech

PROFESSOR ANDERS OLSSON

37

# Opening Address

*Professor Carl-Henrik Heldin*

Your Majesties, your Royal Highnesses, esteemed Nobel Prize laureates, ladies and gentlemen,

On behalf of the Nobel Foundation, it is a great pleasure for me to welcome you all to this year's Nobel Prize award ceremony. In particular, I wish to welcome the Nobel Prize laureates, from 2022 as well as the two previous years, and their families.

This year is special. Since the coronavirus pandemic prevented us from holding regular festivities these two past years, we are now all the happier this year to see the stage filled with Nobel Prize laureates. This gives us a tremendous opportunity to celebrate science and culture, and we are very glad to see you all here in Stockholm!

Earlier today, in Oslo, the prisoner of conscience and human rights advocate Ales Bialiatski, from Belarus; the Russian human rights organization Memorial; and the Ukrainian human rights organization Center for Civil Liberties received this year's Nobel Peace Prize. For many years, they have promoted the right to criticize those in power and to protect the fundamental rights of citizens, emphasizing the significance of civil society for peace and democracy.

In Oslo and Stockholm, we meet today at a time when freedom is in decline globally; when there is war in Europe, even with the specter of nuclear weapons; with dramatic energy and food crises across the world; with glaring discrimination, social and economic inequality, and accelerating climate change, which requires the urgent scaling up of solutions.

Facing this multitude of crises and challenges, the world needs dedicated scientists who relentlessly seek the truth and push the boundaries of our knowledge. And the world needs those individuals and groups which—at great personal sacrifice—challenge authorities in pursuit of peace, democracy, and human rights.

The Nobel Prize is awarded to individuals for concrete achievements in science, literature, and peace, but with a higher, shared purpose: their benefit to humankind. Nobel Prize laureates are part of a community which has, in profound ways, changed the world. They demonstrate the capacity we have as human beings to shape our own destiny.

As such, the Nobel Prize, its laureates, and their achievements are a tremendous source of inspiration and hope, which today is needed more than ever. And the universal ambition to serve the benefit of humankind is also needed more than ever. This is our guiding star when the Nobel Foundation, with generous support from the Erling-Persson Foundation and the Knut and Alice Wallenberg Foundation, now prepares for the future Nobel Center—a house for science, culture, and dialogue to be located at Slussen, here in Stockholm.

In his will, Alfred Nobel directed that the prizes be awarded to those who had conferred the greatest benefit to humankind, regardless of nationality. This was radical and visionary in the late nine-teenth century, an era marked by nationalism—a phenomenon which, sadly, is on the offensive in many countries even today.

But time has proven Alfred Nobel's vision to be powerful. It is indeed the open exchange between countries and cultures that promotes human progress, free science, free culture, humanism, and internationalism.

Today we are celebrating the 2022 Nobel Prizes. They are being awarded for scientific breakthroughs that span from intricate and mindboggling evidence that particles can be entangled despite being at a far distance from each other; to elegant solutions to simplify chemical reactions by click chemistry, facilitating the synthesis of medicines and allowing the monitoring of biological processes in living cells; to insights into how to minimize the risks for financial crises; and to genomic analyses of extinct hominins which have given us invaluable information about human evolution. We also celebrate literature which uncovers the roots, estrangements and collective restraints of personal memory.

Allow me to close by addressing all the laureates from 2020 and 2021, absent or present. You have long since received your medals and diplomas, but we would like to take this occasion to honor you with a musical piece commissioned by the Nobel Foundation. I invite you all to enjoy the world premiere of "Laus Canticum," a song of praise by the Swedish composer Andrea Tarrodi.

*—Opening Address given by Professor Carl-Henrik Heldin, chairman of the board of the Nobel Foundation, December 10, 2022, Stockholm.*

Nobel Lecture

# *I Will Write to Avenge My People*

*Annie Ernaux*

Where to begin? I have asked myself this question dozens of times, gazing at a blank page. As if I needed to find the one, the only sentence that would give me entry into the writing of the book and remove all doubts in one fell swoop—a sort of key. Today, as I confront a situation which, the initial stupor having passed—"Is it really me this is happening to?"—my imagination represents in a way that instills a growing terror, I am overwhelmed by the same necessity: finding the sentence that will give me the freedom and the firmness to speak without trembling in this place to which you have invited me this evening.

To find that sentence, I don't have to look very

far. It instantly appears, in all its clarity and violence: lapidary, irrefutable. Written in my diary sixty years ago: "I will write to avenge my people"—"*J'écrirai pour venger ma race.*" It echoed Rimbaud's cry: "I am of an inferior race for all eternity." I was twenty-two, studying literature in a provincial university with the daughters and sons of the local bourgeoisie, for the most part. I proudly and naively believed that writing books, becoming a writer, as the last in a line of landless laborers, factory workers, and shopkeepers—people despised for their manners, their accent, their lack of education—would be enough to redress the social injustice linked to social class at birth. That an individual victory could erase centuries of domination and poverty—an illusion that school had already fostered in me by dint of my academic success. How could my personal achievement have redeemed any of the humiliations and offenses suffered? That's not a question I ever asked myself. I had a few excuses.

From the time I could read, books were my companions, and reading was my natural occupation outside of school. This appetite was nurtured by a mother who, between customers in her shop, read a great many novels, and preferred me reading rather than sewing and knitting. The high cost of books, the suspicion with which they were regarded at my religious school, made them even more desirable. *Don Quixote*, *Gulliver's Travels*, *Jane Eyre*, the tales of Grimm and Andersen, *David Copperfield*, *Gone with the Wind*, and later *Les Misérables*, *The Grapes of Wrath*, *Nausea*, *The Stranger*: chance, more than the school's prescriptions, determined what I read.

By choosing literary studies I elected to remain inside literature, which had become the thing of greatest value, even a way of life that led me to project myself into the novels of Flaubert or Virginia Woolf and literally live them out. Literature was a sort of continent which I unconsciously set in opposition to my social environment. And I conceived of writing as nothing less than the possibility of transfiguring reality.

It was not the rejection of my first novel by two or three publishers—a novel whose sole merit was its attempt to find a new form—that subdued my desire and my pride. It was life situations in which the weight of difference between a woman's existence and that of a man was keenly felt in a society where roles were defined by gender, where contraception was prohibited and termination of pregnancy a crime. Married with two children, a teaching position, and full responsibility for household affairs, each day I moved further and further away from writing and my promise to avenge my people. I could not read the parable "Before the Law" from Kafka's *The Trial* without seeing in it the shape of my own destiny: to die without ever having entered the gate made just for me, the book that only I could write.

But that was without taking account of private and historical circumstance. The death of a father who passed away three days after I arrived home on vacation, a job teaching students from working-class backgrounds similar to my own, protest movements everywhere in the world: all these factors brought me back, through byroads that were unforeseen and proximate to the world of my origins, to my "people," and gave my desire to write a quality of secret and absolute urgency. No more of the illusory "writing about nothing" of my twenties; now, it was a matter of delving into the unspeakable in repressed memory and bringing light to bear on how my people lived— of writing to understand the reasons, inside and outside of myself, that had caused me to be distanced from my origins.

In writing, no choice is self-evident. But those who, as immigrants, no longer speak their parents' language and those who, as class defectors, no longer have quite the same language, think and express themselves with other words, face additional hurdles—a dilemma. They indeed feel the difficulty, even the impossibility of writing in the acquired, dominant language—which they have mastered and admire in works of literature—anything that relates to their world of origin, that first world made up of sensations and words describing daily life, work, one's place in society. On the one hand is the language in which they learned to name things, with its brutality and silences: for example, that of the intimate exchange between a mother and a son in the very beautiful text by Albert Camus, "Between Yes and No." On the other hand are the models of admired, internalized works, those that made that first world open out and to which they feel indebted for their elevation, which they sometimes even considered their true homeland. Mine included Flaubert, Proust, Virginia Woolf. None of them, when I went back to writing, were of any help to me. I had to break with "writing well" and beautiful sentences—the very kind I taught my

students to write—to root out, display, and understand the rift running through me. What came to
me spontaneously was the clamor of a language
that conveyed anger and derision, even crudeness;
a language of excess, insurgent, often used by the
humiliated and offended as their only response to
the memory of others' contempt, of shame and of
shame at feeling shame.

Very quickly too, it seemed self-evident—to the
point that I could not imagine any other way to
start—to anchor the story of the rift in my social
being in the situation that had been mine as a stu-
dent, a revolting situation to which the French
state still condemned women: the need to seek out
clandestine terminations at the hands of backstreet
abortionists. And I wanted to describe everything
that had happened to my girl's body: the discovery
of pleasure, periods. And so, without being aware
of it at the time, that first book, published in 1974,
mapped out the realm in which I would situate my
writing, a realm both social and feminist. Avenging
my people and avenging my sex would, from that
time on, be one and the same thing.

How can one reflect on life without also reflecting
on writing? Without wondering whether writing

reinforces or disrupts the accepted, interiorized rep-
resentations of beings and things? With its violence
and derision, did insurgent writing not reflect the
attitude of the dominated? When the reader was cul-
turally privileged, he maintained the same imposing
and condescending outlook on a character in a book
as he would in real life. Therefore, originally, it was
to elude this kind of gaze—which, when directed
at my father whose story I was going to tell, would
have been unbearable and, I felt, a betrayal—that,
starting with my fourth book, I adopted a neutral,
objective kind of writing, "flat" in the sense that it
contained neither metaphors nor signs of emotion.
The violence was no longer displayed; it came from
the facts themselves and not the writing. Finding the
words that contain both reality and the sensation
provided by reality would become, and remain to
this day, my ongoing concern in writing, no matter
what the subject.

It was necessary for me to continue to say "I."
In literary use, the first person—the one through
which we exist, in most languages, from the moment
we know how to speak until death—is often considered narcissistic when referring to the author
rather than an "I" presented as fictitious. It is worth

remembering that the "I," hitherto the privilege of nobles recounting feats of arms in memoirs, was in France a democratic conquest of the eighteenth century, the affirmation of the equality of individuals and the right to be the subject of their story, as claimed by Jean-Jacques Rousseau in this first preamble to the *Confessions*: "And let no one object that, being a man of the people, I have nothing to say that deserves the attention of readers. . . . In whatever obscurity I may have lived, if I thought more and better than the Kings, the story of my soul is more interesting than that of theirs."

It was not this plebeian pride that motivated me (although, having said that . . .) but the desire to use the "I"—a form both masculine and feminine—as an exploratory tool that captures sensations: those that memory has buried, those that the world around us keeps on giving, everywhere and all the time. The prerequisite of sensation has for me become both the guide and guarantee of the authenticity of my research. But to what end? Not to tell the story of my life nor free myself of its secrets but to decipher a lived situation, an event, a romantic relationship, and thereby reveal something that only writing can bring into being and perhaps pass on to the consciousness and memories of others. Who could say that love, pain and mourning, shame, are not universal? Victor Hugo wrote: "Not one of us has the honor of living a life that is only his own." But as all things are lived inexorably in the individual mode—"It is to me this is happening"—they can only be read in the same way if the "I" of the book becomes transparent, in a sense, and the "I" of the reader comes to occupy it; if this "I," to put it another way, becomes transpersonal, if singular becomes universal.

This is how I conceived my commitment to writing, which does not consist of writing *for* a category of readers but in writing *from* my experience as a woman and an immigrant of the interior, and from my longer and longer memory of the years I have lived, and from the present, an endless provider of the images and words of others. This commitment through which I pledge myself in writing is supported by the belief, which has become a certainty, that a book can contribute to change in private life, help to shatter the loneliness of experiences endured and repressed, and enable beings to reimagine themselves. When the unspeakable is brought to light, it is political.

We see it today in the revolt of women who have found the words to disrupt male power and who have risen up, as in Iran, against its most violent and archaic form. Writing in a democratic country, however, I continue to wonder about the place women occupy in the literary field. They have not yet gained legitimacy as producers of written works. There are, in France and everywhere in the world, men for whom books written by women simply do not exist; they never cite them. The recognition of my work by the Swedish Academy is a sign of hope for all female writers.

In the bringing to light of the social unspeakable—of those internalized power relations linked to class and/or race, and gender too, felt only by the people who directly experience their impact— the possibility of individual but also collective emancipation emerges. To decipher the real world by stripping it of the visions and values that language, all language, carries within it is to upend its established order, upset its hierarchies.

But I do not confuse the political action of literary writing, subject to its reception by the reader, with the positions I feel compelled to take with respect to events, conflicts, and ideas. I grew up as part of the postwar generation, following World War II, when writers and intellectuals positioned themselves in relation to French politics and became involved in social struggles as a matter of course. Today, it is impossible to say whether things would have turned out differently had they not spoken out and committed themselves. In today's world, where the multiplicity of information sources and the speed at which images flash past condition a form of indifference, to focus on one's art is a temptation. But, meanwhile, in Europe, an ideology of withdrawal and closure is on the rise, still concealed by the violence of an imperialist war waged by the dictator at the head of Russia, and steadily gaining ground in hitherto democratic countries. Founded on the exclusion of foreigners and immigrants, the abandonment of the economically weak, the surveillance of women's bodies, this ideology requires a duty of extreme vigilance, for me and all those for whom the value of a human being is always and everywhere the same. As for the burden of saving the planet, destroyed largely by the limitless appetite of the great economic powers, it cannot fall, as is already to be feared, on those who are already destitute. At such moments in history, silence is not an option.

By granting me the highest literary distinction that can be, a bright light is being shone on work that consists of writing and personal research carried out in solitude and doubt. This light does not dazzle me. I do not regard as an individual victory the Nobel Prize that has been awarded me. It is neither from pride nor modesty that I see it, in some sense, as a collective victory. I share the pride of it with those who, in one way or another, hope for greater freedom, equality, and dignity for all humans, regardless of their sex or gender, the color of their skin, and their culture; and with those who think of future generations, of safeguarding an Earth where a profit-hungry few make life increasingly unlivable for all populations.

If I look back on the promise made at twenty to avenge my people, I cannot say whether I have carried it out. It was from this promise, and from my forebears—hardworking men and women inured to tasks that caused them to die early—that I received enough strength and anger to have the desire and ambition to give them a place in literature, amid this ensemble of voices that, from very early on, accompanied me, giving me access to other worlds and other ways of being, including that of rebelling against and wanting to change it, in order to inscribe my voice as a woman and a social defector in what still presents itself as a space of emancipation: literature.

—*Nobel Lecture given by Annie Ernaux, December 7, 2022, Stockholm. Translated by Alison L. Strayer.*

*Arthur Rimbaud,* A Season in Hell; Une saison en enfer *and* The Drunken Boat; Le bateau ivre. *Translated from the French by Louise Varèse; preface by Patti Smith. New York: New Directions, 2011.*

*Quotations from the following works are translated by Alison L. Strayer: Jean-Jacques Rousseau,* Œuvres complètes I. Les confessions; Autres textes autobiographiques. *Édition publiée sous la direction de Bernard Gagnebin et Marcel Raymond. Paris: Gallimard, 1959; Victor Hugo,* Œuvres complètes. *Poésie V, Les Contemplations (Préface des Contemplations). Paris: Hetzel-Quantin, 1882.*

# Banquet Speech

*Annie Ernaux*

Your Majesties, your Royal Highnesses, Excellencies, dear laureates, ladies and gentlemen,

I was seventeen, in 1957, when I heard on the radio that Albert Camus had been awarded the Nobel Prize in Literature in Stockholm. So I discovered, with a mixture of pride and delight, that the author of *The Stranger* and *The Rebel*, two texts that had deeply affected me, had just been honored by the greatest arbiter of distinction in the world. To find myself here, sixty-five years later, fills me with a sense of profound amazement and gratitude. Amazement at the mystery presented by a life's trajectory and the uncertain, solitary pursuit of its writing. Gratitude for allowing me to join Camus and those other writers, living and dead, whom I admire.

I would also like to thank you on behalf of those who are not here, those men and women who have on occasion discovered in my books some reasons to live and to push back, reasons to feel proud once more. By thus rewarding my work, you compel me to work with even greater determination in search of a reality and a truth that we may share.

*—Banquet Speech given by Annie Ernaux, December 10, 2022, Stockholm. Translated by Sophie Lewis.*

# Presentation Speech

*Professor Anders Olsson*

Your Majesties, your Royal Highnesses, esteemed Nobel Prize laureates, esteemed Nobel Prize laureates in literature for 2020 and 2021, ladies and gentlemen!

There is a question that increasingly occupies contemporary literature: What does writing about one's own life signify? Where is the delineation between "fiction" and "reality"? Few have tackled the issue with the commitment of Annie Ernaux. Charged by the words of poet Arthur Rimbaud—"*Je suis de race inférieure de toute éternité*" ("I am of an inferior race for all eternity.")—she determined early on to rehabilitate the social class she rose from. Driving her is a force and a demand for justice, but instead of emulating the poet's language of imagination to transfigure reality, she chose a different path. For Ernaux, language is a means to dispel the fog of memory and a knife to uncover the real.

Her debut from 1974, *Cleaned Out*, was the commencement of Annie Ernaux's study of her maturation in the little Normandy community of Yvetot, a work of reconstruction that has endured in her writing. The first three books were still narrative accounts labeled "novels," and in the impassioned debut, the twenty-year-old main character, fleeing from her social constraints, is a fictitious character called Denise Lesur. But Ernaux soon abandoned her fictional devices. She has said that her debut work could equally have been called *Getting Rid of Annie Duchesne*—her maiden name. This is revelatory regarding her ambitions. Ernaux always writes autobiographically, in a wider sense, setting the ego in a larger social and historical context. In her most elaborated work, *The Years*, it results in what has been called "collective autobiography," written not in the first person but in the third, and where her own life story fuses with the development of French society over six decades.

Annie Ernaux's breakthrough came with *A Man's Place*, in its brevity a masterful portrait of her father and the working-class background that marked him. The book could be written only from the other side of the class barrier she was forced to transgress to become the writer she is. She writes in solidarity with her father to overcome her self-perceived treachery against his world. The language is as received, with her father's simple phrases seemingly engraved in the strictly factual text. Ernaux's vision is double, aware to what she has witnessed as a daughter but also revealing the distance she has, with time, accrued. In *A Woman's Story*, she writes about her mother in prose as harsh as it is perceptive, as later in *L'Autre fille* about the sister who died young of diphtheria before Annie knew her and was never spoken of by their parents. This extraordinary book, written in the form of a letter to her sister, bears a strong inner drama, wherein Ernaux tries to reconcile the absence of her sister.

Annie Ernaux's writing is restrained with feelings and expressions of emotion, but passion pulses beneath the surface. Relentlessly, Ernaux exposes the shame that penetrates class experience. This occurs in *Shame*, where her father's situation is exposed in scenes that are as suffused with violence as they are humiliating, and from another direction in her depiction of her illegal abortion at the age of twenty-three, in *Happening*, so devastating in its succinctness and controlled rage. She has written: "I have always desired to write books that would be impossible to talk about, that make the gaze of the other unbearable."

An unrelenting gaze and a plain style are Annie Ernaux's characteristics, and that she succeeds in making her pain relevant to all.

Dear Annie Ernaux, allow me to convey the warm congratulations of the Swedish Academy, while asking you to step forward to receive from the hand of his Majesty the King the Nobel Prize in Literature.

*—Presentation Speech given by Professor Anders Olsson, member of the Swedish Academy, chairman of the Nobel Committee for Literature, December 10, 2022, Stockholm. Translated by Kim Loughran.*